BOOK 1

A Good Start Reading

Short "a" Words

Ribbon Star Press

You too can teach your child to read!

Copyright © 2024 by Next Door Creations, LLC
www.olikidsco.com

All rights reserved. No part of this book may be reproduced by any means without written permission of the publisher.

For information regarding written permission, write to:

Ribbon Star Press
2842 Main Street #110
Glastonbury, CT 06033

ISBN 978-0-9909857-5-4

Published by Ribbon Star Press, a division of Next Door Creations, LLC.
Oliver Poons, Oli Kids Co. and associated logos are trademarks of Next Door Creations, LLC.

This Book Belongs to:

....

Letter to Parents & Teachers

"A Good Start" is designed to be the beginning foundation that your child needs to become a strong reader, writer, and speller. It may be used prior to the instructional books and resources in your homeschool program or alongside your homeschool program. "A Good Start" was created to give parents a program to jump start and unlock their child's understanding of how we learn to read, as well as an instructional guide for teaching beginning reading.

We have presented the material in a clear, logical, and sequential order. Previously learned skills are reinforced as the next skill set is learned.

We have organized "A Good Start" through years of teaching experience, so you no longer have to try to figure out what to do. We realize that teaching reading can be both tricky and confusing.

Using this format, you will need to follow the sequence as presented in Books 1-5, allowing your child as much time as needed in each learning area. Of course, continue reading books to and with your child for learning and enjoyment throughout the use of this program.

This instructional book will give you the directions and the tools you need to teach beginner readers short "a" words.

When this material is mastered, continue by teaching short "e" beginner reading words in the next book.

Distinguishing Between "b" and "d"

Distinguishing between lowercase "b" and "d" can be confusing for new readers. Use any or all of these helpful strategies:

1. Make a "b" with your left hand by making a fist with your 4 fingers and sticking your thumb up in the air. Using your right hand, follow the same procedure to made a "d" shape.

Teach the child to make a "b" shape with his or her left hand and a "d" shape with his or her right hand, and use this strategy as confusion arises.

2. Make a circle by connecting your left thumb and index finger, while leaving the remaining three fingers upright. Using your right hand, follow the same procedure to make a "d" shape.

Teach the child to make a "b" shape with his or her left hand and a "d" shape with his or her right hand, and use this strategy as confusion arises.

Distinguishing Between "b" and "d"

3. When confusion arises, remind the child to visualize a top on lowercase "b" (to form an uppercase "B".) If the letter is a lowercase "d", the top doesn't fit and the letter is a "d", not a "b".

4. If the child can write the alphabet, demonstrate that a lowercase "h" can be closed at the bottom to make a "b". Think "h" for "honey" and "b" for "bee".

5. The child can wear a bracelet on their "b" hand since "bracelet" begins with the letter "b". This can help them to remember which hand is their "b" hand. A sticker or a washable magic marker dot on the child's "b" hand is another option.

Practice "b" and "d"

Ask the child to identify each letter for practice distinguishing lowercase "b" and "d". You may want to cut this sheet into strips. Additional copies may be downloaded from our website for more practice.

b　d　b　d

d　b　b　d

b　b　d　b

 Download and print this page as a free printable on www.OliKidsCo.com/downloads.

Practice "b" and "d"

Ask the child to identify each letter for practice distinguishing lowercase "b" and "d". You may want to cut this sheet into strips. Additional copies may be downloaded from our website for more practice.

d b b b

b b d d

d d b d

 Download and print this page as a free printable on www.OliKidsCo.com/downloads.

Book 1 - Short "a" Words

Note: Children should have mastery of the alphabet letters and sounds before proceeding with short "a" words. If you are seeking instructional resources for learning the alphabet, you may purchase our 'Learning the Alphabet' printable downloads on OliKidsCo.com.

The following words are presented for mastery within this program. Upon completion of Book 1, your child will be familiar with the following short **"a"** words:

at	**an**	**ad**	**am**
at	an	ad	am
bat	can	bad	jam
fat	pan	dad	Pam
rat	ran	mad	Sam
cat	tan	sad	ham
hat	fan	had	
sat	van	pad	
mat	man		
pat	Dan		

ap	**ag**	**ax**	**ab**
cap	bag	ax	cab
gap	rag	tax	jab
lap	sag	wax	lab
map	wag	Max	tab
nap	tag		
rap			
tap			
zap			

Vowel Card Short "a"

Place the short **"a"** vowel card on the table for all lessons in this book.

Download and print this vowel card as a free printable on www.OliKidsCo.com/downloads.

Lesson 1

Learning to Read "at" Words

> at   bat   fat   rat   cat
> hat   sat   mat   pat

Students learn mastery of the **"at"** words listed above using the following lessons:

- 1A. Word Formation
- 1B. Cup Game*
- 1C. Flip Cards Game*
- 1D. Match Game*
- 1E. Cut Up Words Game*
- 1F. Word Practice #1
- 1G. Word Practice #2
- 1H. Short Story: The Cats**
- 1I. Sentence Practice
- 1J. Word Check

*Games 1B, 1C, 1D, and 1E can be played in any order.
The words: **the, is, to, and, on, and **in** are used in the stories in this book. Say these words for the child until they become familiar.

1A. Word Formation

1. Place the short **"a"** vowel card on the table for reference.
2. Download and print our **"at"** letter cards (or make your own).
3. Teach a says **"a"**, t says **"t"**.
4. Teach **"a"** and **"t"** together say **"at"**.
5. Teach and show that by moving a letter and placing it in front of **"at"** that a new word is formed (bat, fat, rat, etc.).
6. Change the beginning letter to form different words.

b	f	r
c	at	h
s	m	p

Download and print this activity as a free printable on www.OliKidsCo.com/downloads.

1B. Cup Game

Materials: Plastic cups and permanent markers, or plastic cups, paper, markers, and tape.

1. Using plastic cups, write **"at"** on one cup (or tape it on). Write or tape each of the following letters on separate cups: **b, f, r, c, h, s, m, p**.
2. Instruct the child to find the cup that says **"at"**.
3. Instruct the child to make the word **"cat"** by finding the correct beginning letter among the remaining cups.
4. If needed, use a different color marker for **"at"** than for the single letters.
5. Repeat by asking the child to make a new word by changing the first letter of the word to form different words (bat, fat, rat, etc.).

1C. Flip Cards Game

Materials: Index cards, markers

1. Write "**at**" on an index card.
2. Write the letters **b, f, r, c, h, s, m, p** on separate index cards.
3. You can use a different color for "**at**" and a different color for the letters to alleviate any confusion. Example: Write "at" in red and all other letters in black.
4. Place the "**at**" card on the table.
5. Place all other letter cards in a pile in front of "**at**".
6. Ask the child to read the first word. Then remove the beginning consonant card, replace it with a new consonant, and have the child read the next word.
7. You may use a timer as a challenge.

1D. Play Match Game

Materials: Index cards, markers

1. Using index cards, write out two cards for each of the words in this lesson (**at, bat, fat, rat, cat, hat, sat, mat, and pat**).
2. Shuffle all of the cards and place them face down on the table so all the words are hidden.
3. Decide which player will go first.
4. Each player will take a turn flipping over two cards and reading the word on each card.
5. When a player gets a match, they keep their cards and have another turn.
6. Cards that don't match get placed back where they were and the second player takes a turn.
7. When no cards remain on the table, the player with the most matches is the winner.

I love Match Game! Who will win?

1E. Play Cut Up Words

Materials: Index cards, markers

1. Write a reading word on an index card with space between the letters. Example: c a t
2. Cut the word up so you have 3 pieces.
3. Mix up the letters and ask the child to place the letters in the correct order to spell the word. Example: **"cat"**.
4. Variation: Your child can cut up a word from the **"at"** word list for you to solve too!

Note Before Moving Ahead

It takes a lot of repetition for new readers to learn to read. Move slightly ahead with the sequential lessons and then back to playing games until all the letter sounds and words are mastered. Repetition is the key. Refer to the short **"a"** vowel card frequently, which should be on the table for all lessons.

Myrtle's Reminder:

New skills take time. Go slow and steady.

Repeat, repeat, repeat!

1F. Word Practice #1

Directions

1. Point to the words **at, cat, at, sat, bat** as you read line #1 on the next page.
2. Ask the child to repeat after you as you read the words again.
3. Ask the child to read each word as you point to each word in a left to right sequence. Assist as needed.
4. As the child makes errors, refer to the short **"a"** vowel card on the table. Remind the child that the letter **"a"** says **"a"** like in apple. Point to the letter **"a"** in each word.
5. The word lists can be cut into strips so that just one line is presented at a time. The word lists can be covered with a blank sheet of paper so that only one line at a time can be seen.
6. Move ahead if these words are mastered, or repeat lessons for repetition.

1F. Word Practice #1

1. at   cat   at   sat   bat

2. at   fat   at   hat   mat

3. at   pat   at   mat   cat

4. at   hat   at   rat   sat

5. bat   fat   rat   cat   mat

Checking In

Continue having the child read the word lists and short **"a"** word stories. Continue to play games as needed. Making learning to read into a game format makes learning to read fun. Take the time needed for mastery before moving to the next section.

1G. Word Practice #2

1. at   cat   bat   fat   rat

2. sat   rat   pat   mat   cat

3. hat   bat   cat   sat   fat

4. pat   at   fat   hat   mat

1H. Short Story

The Cats

The cat sat.

The fat cat sat.

The cats sat.

1I. Sentence Practice

1. The fat cat sat on a hat.

2. The fat rat sat on a mat.

3. The rat and cat sat on a mat.

1J. Word Check

Ask the child to read the listed words on the next page. Use your copy (below) to check off the words read correctly and to take any notes about words that need review.

	✓	NOTES
1. at		
2. bat		
3. fat		
4. rat		
5. cat		
6. hat		
7. sat		
8. mat		
9. pat		

IJ. Word Check

1. at
2. bat
3. fat
4. rat
5. cat
6. hat
7. sat
8. mat
9. pat

Lesson 2

Learning to Read "an" Words

> an   can   pan   ran   tan
> fan   van   man   Dan

Students learn mastery of the **"an"** words listed above and reinforce **"at"** words using the following lessons:

2A. Word Formation
2B. Cup Game*
2C. Flip Cards Game*
2D. Match Game*
2E. Cut Up Words Game*
2F. Word Practice #1
2G. Word Practice #2
2H. Sentence Practice
2I. Alternating Word Practice: "at" and "an"
2J. Mixed Word Practice: "at" and "an"
2K. Mixed Sentence Practice: "at" and "an"
2L. Short Story: Dan and the Cat
2M. Word Check

*Games 2B, 2C, 2D, and 2E can be played in any order.

Words to Use in Lesson 2 Games

Combine **"at"** words learned in Lesson 1 with **"an"** words introduced in Lesson 2 to reinforce existing skills and build confidence. As you play Cup Game, Flip Cards Game, Match Game, and Cut Up Words Game, use the following word lists:

<u>at</u>	<u>an</u>
at	an
bat	can
fat	pan
rat	ran
cat	tan
hat	fan
sat	van
mat	man
pat	Dan

2A. Word Formation

1. Place the short **"a"** vowel card on the table for reference.
2. Download and print our **"an"** letter cards (or make your own).
3. Teach a says **"a"**, n says **"n"**.
4. Teach **"a"** and **"n"** together say **"an"**.
5. Teach and show that by moving a letter and placing it in front of **"an"** that a new word is formed (can, pan, ran, etc.).
6. Change the beginning letter to form different words.

c	p	r
t	an	f
v	m	D

Download and print this activity as a free printable on www.OliKidsCo.com/downloads.

2B. Cup Game

Materials: Plastic cups and permanent markers, or plastic cups, paper, markers, and tape.

1. Using plastic cups, write **"an"** on one cup (or tape it on). Write or tape each of the following letters on separate cups: **c, p, r, t, f, v, m, D**.
2. Instruct the child to find the cup that says **"an"**.
3. Instruct the child to make the word **"can"** by finding the correct beginning letter among the remaining cups.
4. If needed, use a different color marker for **"an"** than for the single letters.
5. Repeat by asking the child to make a new word by changing the first letter of the word to form different words (pan, ran, tan, etc.).

2C. Flip Cards Game

Materials: Index cards, markers

1. Write "**an**" on an index card.
2. Write the letters **c, p, r, t, f, v, m, D** on separate index cards.
3. You can use a different color for "**an**" and a different color for the letters to alleviate any confusion. Example: Write "**an**" in red and all other letters in black.
4. Place the "**an**" card on the table.
5. Place all other letter cards in a pile in front of "**an**".
6. Ask the child to read the first word. Then remove the beginning consonant card, replace it with a new consonant, and have the child read the next word.
7. You may use a timer as a challenge.

2D. Play Match Game

Materials: Index cards, markers

1. Using index cards, write out two cards for each of the words in this lesson (**an, can, pan, ran, tan, fan, van, man, Dan**).
2. You can either play match game with only the words introduced in this lesson or add in words from the previous lesson. See the word list to use in games at the beginning of this lesson.
3. Shuffle all of the cards and place them face down on the table so all the words are hidden.
4. Decide which player will go first.
5. Each player will take a turn flipping over two cards and reading the word on each card.
6. When a player gets a match, they keep their cards and have another turn.
7. Cards that don't match get placed back where they were and the second player takes a turn.
8. When no cards remain on the table, the player with the most matches is the winner.

I love Match Game! Who will win?

2E. Play Cut Up Words

Materials: Index cards, markers

1. Write a reading word on an index card with space between the letters. Example: c a n
2. Cut the word up so you have 3 pieces.
3. Mix up the letters and ask the child to place the letters in the correct order to spell the word. Example: **"can"**.
4. Variation: Your child can cut up a word from the **"an"** word list for you to solve too!
5. You may use any or all of the words you have taught up until this point. Refer to the word list for games included at the beginning of this lesson.

Note Before Moving Ahead

It takes a lot of repetition for new readers to learn to read. Move slightly ahead with the sequential lessons and then back to playing games until all the letter sounds and words are mastered. Repetition is the key. Refer to the short **"a"** vowel card frequently, which should be on the table for all lessons.

Myrtle's Reminder:

New skills take time. Go slow and steady.

Repeat, repeat, repeat!

2F. Word Practice #1

Directions

1. Point to the words **an, can, an, pan, ran** as you read line #1 on the next page.
2. Ask the child to repeat after you as you read the words again.
3. Ask the child to read each word as you point to each word in a left to right sequence. Assist as needed.
4. As the child makes errors, refer to the short **"a"** vowel card on the table. Remind the child that the letter **"a"** says **"a"** like in apple. Point to the letter **"a"** in each word.
5. The word lists can be cut into strips so that just one line is presented at a time. The word lists can be covered with a blank sheet of paper so that only one line at a time can be seen.
6. Move ahead if these words are mastered, or repeat lessons for repetition.

2F. Word Practice #1

1. an   can   an   pan   ran

2. an   tan   an   man   Dan

3. an   fan   an   ran   can

4. an   van   an   tan   man

5. tan   man   ran   can   Dan

Checking In

Continue having the child read the word lists and short **"a"** word stories. Continue to play games as needed. Making learning to read into a game format makes learning to read fun. Take the time needed for mastery before moving to the next section.

2G. Word Practice #2

1. can pan ran tan fan

2. fan van man Dan tan

3. can Dan van ran pan

4. tan man pan Dan tan

5. man tan ran pan can

2H. Sentence Practice

Directions: Practice **"at"** and **"an"** words.

1. Dan and a man ran.

2. The tan cat sat.

3. The fan is tan.

4. The man ran to the van.

2I. Alternating Word Practice

Directions: Practice **"at"** and **"an"** words.

1. at   bat   fat   rat   cat

2. an   can   ran   tan   fan

3. hat   sat   mat   pat   cat

4. Dan   man   van   fan   pan

5. cat   sat   hat   rat   fat

6. tan   ran   pan   can   van

2J. Mixed Word Practice

Directions: Practice **"at"** and **"an"** words when mixed together.

1. at   can   bat   pan   ran

2. fat   hat   man   mat   rat

3. hat   sat   mat   pat   cat

4. Dan   man   van   fan   pan

5. cat   sat   hat   rat   fat

6. tan   ran   pan   can   van

2K. Mixed Sentence Practice

1. The fat cat and rat ran.

2. The man and the cat sat on the mat.

3. Dan and the tan cat ran.

4. Dan can bat.

2L. Short Story

Dan and the Cat

Dan ran.

Dan ran to the fat cat.

Dan sat. The cat sat. Dan and the fat cat sat on a mat.

Move to the next page to begin the word check.

2M. Word Check

Ask the child to read the listed words on the next page. Use your copy (below) to check off the words read correctly and to take any notes about words that need review.

	✓	NOTES
1. an		
2. can		
3. pan		
4. ran		
5. tan		
6. fan		
7. van		
8. man		
9. Dan		

2M. Word Check

1. an
2. can
3. pan
4. ran
5. tan
6. fan
7. van
8. man
9. Dan

Lesson 3

Learning to Read "ad" Words

> ad   bad   dad   mad
> sad   had   pad

Students learn mastery of the **"ad"** words listed above and reinforce **"at"** and **"an"** words using the following lessons:

3A. Word Formation
3B. Cup Game*
3C. Flip Cards Game*
3D. Match Game*
3E. Cut Up Words Game*
3F. Word Practice #1
3G. Word Practice #2
3H Mixed Word Practice: **"an"** and **"ad"**
3I. Mixed Word Practice #1 : **"at"**, **"an"** and **"ad"**
3J. Mixed Word Practice #2 : **"at"**, **"an"** and **"ad"**
3K. Short Story: The Tan Cat Ran
3L. Word Check

*Games 3B, 3C, 3D, and 3E can be played in any order.

Words to Use in Lesson 3 Games

Combine **"at"** and **"an"** words learned in Lessons 1 and 2 with **"ad"** words introduced in Lesson 3 to reinforce existing skills and build confidence. As you play Cup Game, Flip Cards Game, Match Game, and Cut Up Words Game, use the following word lists:

<u>at</u>	<u>an</u>	<u>ad</u>
at	an	ad
bat	can	bad
fat	pan	dad
rat	ran	mad
cat	tan	sad
hat	fan	had
sat	van	pad
mat	man	
pat	Dan	

3A. Word Formation

1. Place the short **"a"** vowel card on the table for reference.
2. Download and print our **"ad"** letter cards (or make your own).
3. Teach a says **"a"**, d says **"d"**.
4. Teach **"a"** and **"d"** together say **"ad"**.
5. Teach and show that by moving a letter and placing it in front of **"ad"** that a new word is formed (had, pad, bad, dad, etc.).
6. Change the beginning letter to form different words.

h	p	b
	ad	m
s		d

Download and print this activity as a free printable on www.OliKidsCo.com/downloads.

3B. Cup Game

Materials: Plastic cups and permanent markers, or plastic cups, paper, markers, and tape.

1. Using plastic cups, write **"ad"** on one cup (or tape it on). Write or tape each of the following letters on separate cups: **h, p, b, m, s, d**.
2. Instruct the child to find the cup that says **"ad"**.
3. Instruct the child to make the word **"mad"** by finding the correct beginning letter among the remaining cups.
4. If needed, use a different color marker for **"ad"** than for the single letters.
5. Repeat by asking the child to make a new word by changing the first letter of the word to form different words (bad, dad, sad, etc.).

3C. Flip Cards Game

Materials: Index cards, markers

1. Write **"ad"** on an index card.
2. Write the letters **h, p, b, m, s, d** on separate index cards.
3. You can use a different color for **"ad"** and a different color for the letters to alleviate any confusion. Example: Write **"ad"** in red and all other letters in black.
4. Place the **"ad"** card on the table.
5. Place all other letter cards in a pile in front of **"ad"**.
6. Ask the child to read the first word. Then remove the beginning consonant card, replace it with a new consonant, and have the child read the next word.
7. You may use a timer as a challenge.

3D. Play Match Game

Materials: Index cards, markers

1. Using index cards, write out two cards for each of the words in this lesson (**ad, had, pad, bad, mad, sad, dad**).
2. You can either play match game with only the words introduced in this lesson or add in words from previous lessons. See the word list to use in games at the beginning of this lesson.
3. Shuffle all of the cards and place them face down on the table so all the words are hidden.
4. Decide which player will go first.
5. Each player will take a turn flipping over two cards and reading the word on each card.
6. When a player gets a match, they keep their cards and have another turn.
7. Cards that don't match get placed back where they were and the second player takes a turn.
8. When no cards remain on the table, the player with the most matches is the winner.

I love Match Game! Who will win?

3E. Play Cut Up Words

Materials: Index cards, markers

1. Write a reading word on an index card with space between the letters. Example: p a d
2. Cut the word up so you have 3 pieces.
3. Mix up the letters and ask the child to place the letters in the correct order to spell the word. Example: **"pad"**.
4. Variation: Your child can cut up a word from the **"ad"** word list for you to solve too!
5. You may use any or all of the words you have taught up until this point. Refer to the word list for games included at the beginning of this lesson.

Note Before Moving Ahead

It takes a lot of repetition for new readers to learn to read. Move slightly ahead with the sequential lessons and then back to playing games until all the letter sounds and words are mastered. Repetition is the key. Refer to the short **"a"** vowel card frequently, which should be on the table for all lessons.

Myrtle's Reminder:

New skills take time. Go slow and steady.

Repeat, repeat, repeat!

3F. Word Practice #1

Directions

1. Point to the words **ad, had, mad, ad, sad** as you read line #1 on the next page.
2. Ask the child to repeat after you as you read the words again.
3. Ask the child to read each word as you point to each word in a left to right sequence. Assist as needed.
4. As the child makes errors, refer to the short **"a"** vowel card on the table. Remind the child that the letter **"a"** says **"a"** like in apple. Point to the letter **"a"** in each word.
5. The word lists can be cut into strips so that just one line is presented at a time. The word lists can be covered with a blank sheet of paper so that only one line at a time can be seen.
6. Move ahead if these words are mastered, or repeat lessons for repetition.

3F. Word Practice #1

1. ad   had   mad   ad   sad

2. ad   mad   dad   sad   mad

3. had   bad   mad   pad   had

4. dad   sad   bad   mad   ad

5. bad   dad   pad   sad   ad

Checking In

Continue having the child read the word lists and short **"a"** word stories. Continue to play games as needed. Making learning to read into a game format makes learning to read fun. Take the time needed for mastery before moving to the next section.

3G. Word Practice #2

1. had   ad   bad   dad   mad

2. sad   had   pad   mad   ad

3. dad   pad   had   bad   mad

4. sad   ad   bad   dad   mad

5. had   ad   sad   mad   dad

3H. Mixed Word Practice: "an" and "ad"

Directions: Practice **"an"** and **"ad"** words.

1. ad   had   can   mad   tan

2. pad   pan   tan   bad   man

3. ran   bad   fan   sad   had

4. dad   fan   ad   mad   can

5. van   mad   dad   sad   Dan

6. sad   man   pad   bad   mad

3I. Mixed Word Practice #1: "at", "an" and "ad"

Directions: Practice **"at"**, **"an"** and **"ad"** words.

1. at ad can hat dad mad

2. sat van ad sad bad dad

3. can pat dad mad man pad

4. tan mad hat pan mat van

5. mat ran sad bad had man

6. man an rat ad bad dad

3J. Mixed Word Practice #2: "at", "an" and "ad"

Directions: Practice **"at"**, **"an"** and **"ad"** words.

1. bat pan ad bad cat fat

2. can had fat pad van man

3. rat ran Dan tan mad man

4. tan dad cat hat bad bat

5. sat mad had dad fan tan

6. pat van sad man mat cat

3K. Short Story
The Tan Cat Ran

The tan cat ran.

Dad ran.

Dan ran.

3K. Short Story

 The man ran.

 Dad is mad at the tan cat.

 The tan cat sat.

3K. Short Story

Dad is 🙂. Dan is 🙂. The man is 🙂. The tan cat is 🙂.

3L. Word Check

Ask the child to read the listed words on the next page. Use your copy (below) to check off the words read correctly and to take any notes about words that need review.

Use previous word checks again as needed.

	✓	NOTES
1. ad		
2. bad		
3. dad		
4. mad		
5. sad		
6. had		
7. pad		

3L. Word Check

1. ad
2. bad
3. dad
4. mad
5. sad
6. had
7. pad

Lesson 4

Learning to Read "am" Words

| am   jam   Pam   Sam   ham |

Students learn mastery of the **"am"** words listed above and reinforce **"at"**, **"an"** and **"ad"** words using the following lessons:

4A. Word Formation
4B. Cup Game*
4C. Flip Cards Game*
4D. Match Game*
4E. Cut Up Words Game*
4F. Word Practice #1
4G. Mixed Word Practice #1 : **"am"** and **"an"**
4H. Mixed Word Practice #2 : Short **"a"** Words
4I. Short Story: Ham and Jam
4J. Word Check

*Games 4B, 4C, 4D, and 4E can be played in any order.

Words to Use in Lesson 4 Games

Combine **"at"**, **"an"**, and **"ad"** words learned in Lessons 1, 2, and 3 with **"am"** words introduced in Lesson 4 to reinforce existing skills and build confidence. As you play Cup Game, Flip Cards Game, Match Game, and Cut Up Words Game, use the following word lists:

<u>at</u>	<u>an</u>	<u>ad</u>	<u>am</u>
at	an	ad	am
bat	can	bad	jam
fat	pan	dad	Pam
rat	ran	mad	Sam
cat	tan	sad	ham
hat	fan	had	
sat	van	pad	
mat	man		
pat	Dan		

4A. Word Formation

1. Place the short **"a"** vowel card on the table for reference.
2. Download and print our **"am"** letter cards (or make your own).
3. Teach a says **"a"**, m says **"m"**.
4. Teach **"a"** and **"m"** together say **"am"**.
5. Teach and show that by moving a letter and placing it in front of **"am"** that a new word is formed (jam, Pam, Sam, ham).
6. Change the beginning letter to form different words.

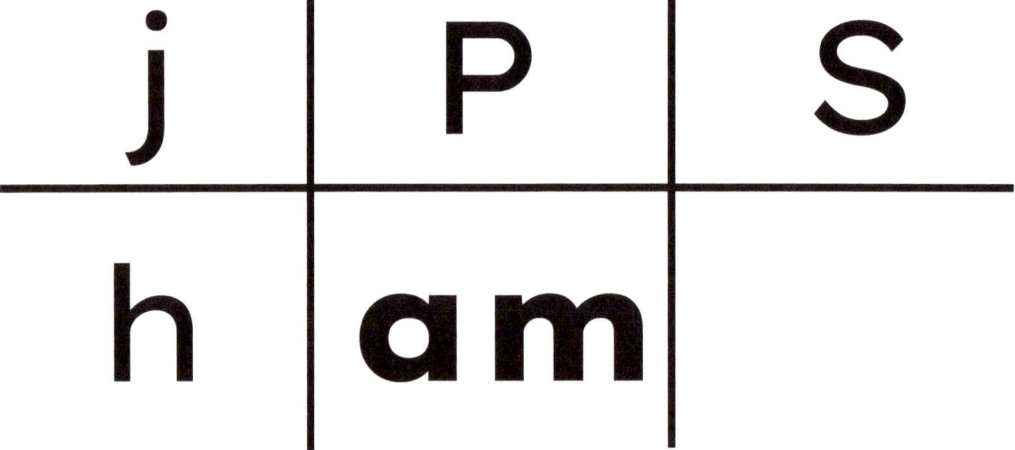

 Download and print this activity as a free printable on www.OliKidsCo.com/downloads.

4B. Cup Game

Materials: Plastic cups and permanent markers, or plastic cups, paper, markers, and tape.

1. Using plastic cups, write **"am"** on one cup (or tape it on). Write or tape each of the following letters on separate cups: **j, P, S, h**.
2. Instruct the child to find the cup that says **"am"**.
3. Instruct the child to make the word **"jam"** by finding the correct beginning letter among the remaining cups.
4. If needed, use a different color marker for **"am"** than for the single letters.
5. Repeat by asking the child to make a new word by changing the first letter of the word to form different words (jam, Pam, Sam, ham).

4C. Flip Cards Game

Materials: Index cards, markers

1. Write "**am**" on an index card.
2. Write the letters **j, P, S, h** on separate index cards.
3. You can use a different color for "**am**" and a different color for the letters to alleviate any confusion. Example: Write "**am**" in red and all other letters in black.
4. Place the "**am**" card on the table.
5. Place all other letter cards in a pile in front of "**am**".
6. Ask the child to read the first word. Then remove the beginning consonant card, replace it with a new consonant, and have the child read the next word.
7. You may use a timer as a challenge.

4D. Play Match Game

Materials: Index cards, markers

1. Using index cards, write out two cards for each of the words in this lesson (**am, jam, Pam, Sam, ham**).
2. You can either play match game with only the words introduced in this lesson or add in words from previous lessons. See the word list to use in games at the beginning of this lesson.
3. Shuffle all of the cards and place them face down on the table so all the words are hidden.
4. Decide which player will go first.
5. Each player will take a turn flipping over two cards and reading the word on each card.
6. When a player gets a match, they keep their cards and have another turn.
7. Cards that don't match get placed back where they were and the second player takes a turn.
8. When no cards remain on the table, the player with the most matches is the winner.

I love Match Game! Who will win?

4E. Play Cut Up Words

Materials: Index cards, markers

1. Write a reading word on an index card with space between the letters. Example: j a m
2. Cut the word up so you have 3 pieces.
3. Mix up the letters and ask the child to place the letters in the correct order to spell the word. Example: **"jam"**.
4. Variation: Your child can cut up a word from the **"am"** word list for you to solve too!
5. You may use any or all of the words you have taught up until this point. Refer to the word list for games included at the beginning of this lesson.

Note Before Moving Ahead

It takes a lot of repetition for new readers to learn to read. Move slightly ahead with the sequential lessons and then back to playing games until all the letter sounds and words are mastered. Repetition is the key. Refer to the short **"a"** vowel card frequently, which should be on the table for all lessons.

Myrtle's Reminder:

New skills take time. Go slow and steady.

Repeat, repeat, repeat!

4F. Word Practice #1

Directions

1. Point to the words **am, jam, Pam, Sam, ham** as you read line #1 on the next page.
2. Ask the child to repeat after you as you read the words again.
3. Ask the child to read each word as you point to each word in a left to right sequence. Assist as needed.
4. As the child makes errors, refer to the short **"a"** vowel card on the table. Remind the child that the letter **"a"** says **"a"** like in apple. Point to the letter **"a"** in each word.
5. The word lists can be cut into strips so that just one line is presented at a time. The word lists can be covered with a blank sheet of paper so that only one line at a time can be seen.
6. Move ahead if these words are mastered, or repeat lessons for repetition.

4F. Word Practice #1

1. am   jam   Pam   Sam   ham

2. jam   am   Sam   Pam   am

3. am   Sam   Pam   jam   ham

4. ham   jam   am   Sam   Pam

5. Pam   am   jam   ham   Sam

Checking In

Continue having the child read the word lists and short **"a"** word stories. Continue to play games as needed. Making learning to read into a game format makes learning to read fun. Take the time needed for mastery before moving to the next section.

4G. Mixed Word Practice #1: "am" and "an"

Directions: Practice **"am"** and **"an"** words.

1. am   an   ran   jam   Pam   pan

2. Sam   pan   ran   ham   jam   Pam

3. fan   jam   ham   van   man   can

4. tan   Pam   Sam   fan   ham   van

5. can   ran   jam   ham   ran   Sam

4H. Mixed Word Practice #2: Short "a" Words

Directions: Practice short **"a"** words introduced in Lessons 1-4.

1. bat can ad mad Pam mat

2. pan jam bad dad sad had

3. fat Pam dad tan hat cat

4. van mat Sam sat ran man

5. pat ham mat sad tan man

6. fan mad pan Dan jam rat

4I. Short Story
Ham and Jam

Pam and Sam had jam.

The fat cat in the hat had ham.

Dad had ham.
Dan had ham.

4J. Word Check

Ask the child to read the listed words on the next page. Use your copy (below) to check off the words read correctly and to take any notes about words that need review.

Use previous word checks again as needed.

	✓	NOTES
1. am		
2. jam		
3. Pam		
4. Sam		
5. ham		

4J. Word Check

1. am
2. jam
3. Pam
4. Sam
5. ham

Lesson 5

Learning to Read "ap" Words

> cap   gap   lap   map   nap
> rap   tap   zap

Students learn mastery of the **"ap"** words listed above and reinforce **"at"**, **"an"**, **"ad"** and **"am"** words using the following lessons:

5A. Word Formation
5B. Cup Game*
5C. Flip Cards Game*
5D. Match Game*
5E. Cut Up Words Game*
5F. Word Practice #1
5G. Mixed Word Practice
5H. Short Sentence Practice
5I. Short Story: A Nap
5J. Word Check

*Games 5B, 5C, 5D, and 5E can be played in any order.

Words to Use in Lesson 5 Games

Combine **"at"**, **"an"**, **"ad"** and **"am"** words learned in Lessons 1-4 with **"ap"** words introduced in Lesson 5 to reinforce existing skills and build confidence. As you play Cup Game, Flip Cards Game, Match Game, and Cut Up Words Game, use the following word lists:

<u>at</u>	<u>an</u>	<u>ad</u>	<u>am</u>
at	an	ad	am
bat	can	bad	jam
fat	pan	dad	Pam
rat	ran	mad	Sam
cat	tan	sad	ham
hat	fan	had	
sat	van	pad	
mat	man		
pat	Dan		

<u>ap</u>

cap
gap
lap
map
nap
rap
tap
zap

5A. Word Formation

1. Place the short **"a"** vowel card on the table for reference.
2. Download and print our **"ap"** letter cards (or make your own).
3. Teach a says **"a"**, p says **"p"**.
4. Teach **"a"** and **"p"** together say **"ap"**.
5. Teach and show that by moving a letter and placing it in front of **"ap"** that a new word is formed (cap, gap, lap, map, etc.).
6. Change the beginning letter to form different words.

c	g	l
m	**ap**	n
r	t	z

Download and print this activity as a free printable on www.OliKidsCo.com/downloads.

5B. Cup Game

Materials: Plastic cups and permanent markers, or plastic cups, paper, markers, and tape.

1. Using plastic cups, write **"ap"** on one cup (or tape it on). Write or tape each of the following letters on separate cups: **c, g, l, m, n, r, t, z**.
2. Instruct the child to find the cup that says **"ap"**.
3. Instruct the child to make the word **"cap"** by finding the correct beginning letter among the remaining cups.
4. If needed, use a different color marker for **"ap"** than for the single letters.
5. Repeat by asking the child to make a new word by changing the first letter of the word to form different words (gap, lap, map, nap, etc.).

5C. Flip Cards Game

Materials: Index cards, markers

1. Write "**ap**" on an index card.
2. Write the letters **c, g, l, m, n, r, t, z** on separate index cards.
3. You can use a different color for "**ap**" and a different color for the letters to alleviate any confusion. Example: Write "**ap**" in red and all other letters in black.
4. Place the "**ap**" card on the table.
5. Place all other letter cards in a pile in front of "**ap**".
6. Ask the child to read the first word. Then remove the beginning consonant card, replace it with a new consonant, and have the child read the next word.
7. You may use a timer as a challenge.

5D. Play Match Game

Materials: Index cards, markers

1. Using index cards, write out two cards for each of the words in this lesson (**cap, gap, lap, map, nap, rap, tap, zap**).
2. You can either play match game with only the words introduced in this lesson or add in words from previous lessons. See the word list to use in games at the beginning of this lesson.
3. Shuffle all of the cards and place them face down on the table so all the words are hidden.
4. Decide which player will go first.
5. Each player will take a turn flipping over two cards and reading the word on each card.
6. When a player gets a match, they keep their cards and have another turn.
7. Cards that don't match get placed back where they were and the second player takes a turn.
8. When no cards remain on the table, the player with the most matches is the winner.

I love Match Game! Who will win?

5E. Play Cut Up Words

Materials: Index cards, markers

1. Write a reading word on an index card with space between the letters. Example: c a p
2. Cut the word up so you have 3 pieces.
3. Mix up the letters and ask the child to place the letters in the correct order to spell the word. Example: **"cap"**.
4. Variation: Your child can cut up a word from the **"ap"** word list for you to solve too!
5. You may use any or all of the words you have taught up until this point. Refer to the word list for games included at the beginning of this lesson.

Note Before Moving Ahead

It takes a lot of repetition for new readers to learn to read. Move slightly ahead with the sequential lessons and then back to playing games until all the letter sounds and words are mastered. Repetition is the key. Refer to the short **"a"** vowel card frequently, which should be on the table for all lessons.

Myrtle's Reminder:

New skills take time. Go slow and steady.

Repeat, repeat, repeat!

5F. Word Practice #1

Directions

1. Point to the words **cap, gap, lap, map, nap** as you read line #1 on the next page.
2. Ask the child to repeat after you as you read the words again.
3. Ask the child to read each word as you point to each word in a left to right sequence. Assist as needed.
4. As the child makes errors, refer to the short **"a"** vowel card on the table. Remind the child that the letter **"a"** says **"a"** like in apple. Point to the letter **"a"** in each word.
5. The word lists can be cut into strips so that just one line is presented at a time. The word lists can be covered with a blank sheet of paper so that only one line at a time can be seen.
6. Move ahead if these words are mastered, or repeat lessons for repetition.

5F. Word Practice #1

1. cap gap lap map nap

2. rap tap zap cap lap

3. map nap rap tap zap

4. gap lap map nap tap

5. cap lap map gap tap

6. lap map cap tap zap

Checking In

Continue having the child read the word lists and short **"a"** word stories. Continue to play games as needed. Making learning to read into a game format makes learning to read fun. Take the time needed for mastery before moving to the next section.

5G. Mixed Word Practice

1. cap   had   fan   van   hat   lap

2. tan   fan   map   had   dad   bat

3. bad   fat   jam   Pam   pad   hat

4. cat   gap   nap   map   tan   fan

5. tap   sat   dad   bad   sad   ham

6. mad   map   ham   Sam   Pam   jam

7. dad   ad   rat   pad   mad   mat

8. Pat   Sam   mat   fat   can   bat

5H. Short "a" Sentence Practice

1. The cat sat on the mat.

2. Pam and Sam had jam.

3. The man and dad ran to the van.

4. The fat cat had a nap on Dad's lap.

5. Dan and Dad had a tan van.

6. Sam is mad and sad.

7. The rat and cat sat on a mat.

8. Sam had a cap.

Move to the next page to begin the short story.

5I. Short Story

A Nap

 Dad had a tan van.

 Dad had a map.

 The tan cat had a nap in the van.

5I. Short Story

Dad had a nap in the van.

Tap! Tap! Tap! Rap! Tap!

It is Sam! Sam is in the van.

5J. Word Check

Ask the child to read the listed words on the next page. Use your copy (below) to check off the words read correctly and to take any notes about words that need review.

Use previous word checks again as needed.

	✓	NOTES
1. cap		
2. gap		
3. lap		
4. map		
5. nap		
6. rap		
7. tap		
8. zap		

5J. Word Check

1. cap
2. gap
3. lap
4. map
5. nap
6. rap
7. tap
8. zap

Lesson 6

Learning to Read "ag" Words

> bag   rag   sag
> wag   tag

Students learn mastery of the **"ag"** words listed above and reinforce **"at"**, **"an"**, **"ad"**, **"am"** and **"ap"** words using the following lessons:

6A. Word Formation
6B. Cup Game*
6C. Flip Cards Game*
6D. Match Game*
6E. Cut Up Words Game*
6F. Word Practice #1
6G. Mixed Word Practice
6H. Short Sentence Practice
6I. Short Story: Rags, Sam, and Dad
6J. Word Check

*Games 6B, 6C, 6D, and 6E can be played in any order.

Words to Use in Lesson 6 Games

Combine **"at"**, **"an"**, **"ad"**, **"am"** and **"ap"** words learned in Lessons 1-5 with **"ag"** words introduced in Lesson 6 to reinforce existing skills and build confidence. As you play Cup Game, Flip Cards Game, Match Game, and Cut Up Words Game, use the following word lists:

<u>at</u>	<u>an</u>	<u>ad</u>	<u>am</u>
at	an	ad	am
bat	can	bad	jam
fat	pan	dad	Pam
rat	ran	mad	Sam
cat	tan	sad	ham
hat	fan	had	
sat	van	pad	
mat	man		
pat	Dan		

<u>ap</u>	<u>ag</u>
cap	bag
gap	rag
lap	sag
map	wag
nap	tag
rap	
tap	
zap	

6A. Word Formation

1. Place the short **"a"** vowel card on the table for reference.
2. Download and print our **"ag"** letter cards (or make your own).
3. Teach a says **"a"**, g says **"g"**.
4. Teach **"a"** and **"g"** together say **"ag"**.
5. Teach and show that by moving a letter and placing it in front of **"ag"** that a new word is formed (bag, rag, wag, etc.).
6. Change the beginning letter to form different words.

r	b	s
w	ag	t

Download and print this activity as a free printable on www.OliKidsCo.com/downloads.

6B. Cup Game

Materials: Plastic cups and permanent markers, or plastic cups, paper, markers, and tape.

1. Using plastic cups, write **"ag"** on one cup (or tape it on). Write or tape each of the following letters on separate cups: **r, b, s, w, t**.
2. Instruct the child to find the cup that says **"ag"**.
3. Instruct the child to make the word **"bag"** by finding the correct beginning letter among the remaining cups.
4. If needed, use a different color marker for **"ag"** than for the single letters.
5. Repeat by asking the child to make a new word by changing the first letter of the word to form different words (rag, wag, sag, etc.).

6C. Flip Cards Game

Materials: Index cards, markers

1. Write "**ag**" on an index card.
2. Write the letters **b, r, s, t, w** on separate index cards.
3. You can use a different color for "**ag**" and a different color for the letters to alleviate any confusion. Example: Write "**ag**" in red and all other letters in black.
4. Place the "**ag**" card on the table.
5. Place all other letter cards in a pile in front of "**ag**".
6. Ask the child to read the first word. Then remove the beginning consonant card, replace it with a new consonant, and have the child read the next word.
7. You may use a timer as a challenge.

6D. Play Match Game

Materials: Index cards, markers

1. Using index cards, write out two cards for each of the words in this lesson (**bag, rag, sag, tag, wag**).
2. You can either play match game with only the words introduced in this lesson or add in words from previous lessons. See the word list to use in games at the beginning of this lesson.
3. Shuffle all of the cards and place them face down on the table so all the words are hidden.
4. Decide which player will go first.
5. Each player will take a turn flipping over two cards and reading the word on each card.
6. When a player gets a match, they keep their cards and have another turn.
7. Cards that don't match get placed back where they were and the second player takes a turn.
8. When no cards remain on the table, the player with the most matches is the winner.

6E. Play Cut Up Words

Materials: Index cards, markers

1. Write a reading word on an index card with space between the letters. Example: b a g
2. Cut the word up so you have 3 pieces.
3. Mix up the letters and ask the child to place the letters in the correct order to spell the word. Example: **"bag"**.
4. Variation: Your child can cut up a word from the **"ag"** word list for you to solve too!
5. You may use any or all of the words you have taught up until this point. Refer to the word list for games included at the beginning of this lesson.

Note Before Moving Ahead

It takes a lot of repetition for new readers to learn to read. Move slightly ahead with the sequential lessons and then back to playing games until all the letter sounds and words are mastered. Repetition is the key. Refer to the short **"a"** vowel card frequently, which should be on the table for all lessons.

Myrtle's Reminder:

New skills take time. Go slow and steady.

Repeat, repeat, repeat!

6F. Word Practice #1

Directions

1. Point to the words **bag, rag, sag, tag, wag** as you read line #1 on the next page.
2. Ask the child to repeat after you as you read the words again.
3. Ask the child to read each word as you point to each word in a left to right sequence. Assist as needed.
4. As the child makes errors, refer to the short **"a"** vowel card on the table. Remind the child that the letter **"a"** says **"a"** like in apple. Point to the letter **"a"** in each word.
5. The word lists can be cut into strips so that just one line is presented at a time. The word lists can be covered with a blank sheet of paper so that only one line at a time can be seen.
6. Move ahead if these words are mastered, or repeat lessons for repetition.

6F. Word Practice #1

1. bag rag sag tag wag

2. tag wag rag bag tag

3. wag rag bag tag sag

4. tag bag sag wag rag

5. bag wag tag rag bag

6. tag sag wag bag rag

Checking In

Continue having the child read the word lists and short **"a"** word stories. Continue to play games as needed. Making learning to read into a game format makes learning to read fun. Take the time needed for mastery before moving to the next section.

6G. Mixed Word Practice

1. wag bat can bag sat sag

2. pan tag jam tag dad mad

3. fat Sam sag rag pad cap

4. tag rat Pam gap mat lap

5. wag bad ran had map nap

6. tan sad tap wag pat fan

7. zap cat ham sad mad had

8. hat fan van mat pat rat

6H. Short "a" Sentence Practice

1. Sam had a rag in a bag.

2. The fat cat had a tag.

3. Dan had a map.

4. The cat sat in Dad's lap.

5. Sam ran to the tan van.

6. Sam had ham and a nap.

7. Pam had a pan.

8. The fat cat had a nap.

Move to the next page to begin the short story.

6I. Short Story
Rags, Sam, and Dad

 Rags had a hat.

 Sam had a hat.

 Dad had a hat.

6I. Short Story

 Rags had a nap.

 Sam had a nap.

 Dad had a nap.

Nap! Nap! Nap!

6J. Word Check

Ask the child to read the listed words on the next page. Use your copy (below) to check off the words read correctly and to take any notes about words that need review.

Use previous word checks again as needed.

	✓	NOTES
1. bag		
2. rag		
3. sag		
4. tag		
5. wag		

6J. Word Check

1. bag
2. rag
3. sag
4. tag
5. wag

Lesson 7

Learning to Read "ax" Words

> ax   tax   wax   Max

Students learn mastery of the **"ax"** words listed above and reinforce **"at"**, **"an"**, **"ad"**, **"am"**, **"ap"** and **"ag"** words using the following lessons:

7A. Word Formation
7B. Cup Game*
7C. Flip Cards Game*
7D. Match Game*
7E. Cut Up Words Game*
7F. Mixed Word Practice #1
7G. Mixed Word Practice #2
7H. Short Sentence Practice
7I. Word Check

*Games 7B, 7C, 7D, and 7E can be played in any order.

Words to Use in Lesson 7 Games

Combine **"at"**, **"an"**, **"ad"**, **"am"**, **"ap"** and **"ag"** words learned in Lessons 1-6 with **"ax"** words introduced in Lesson 7 to reinforce existing skills and build confidence. As you play Cup Game, Flip Cards Game, Match Game, and Cut Up Words Game, use the following word lists:

<u>at</u>	<u>an</u>	<u>ad</u>	<u>am</u>
at	an	ad	am
bat	can	bad	jam
fat	pan	dad	Pam
rat	ran	mad	Sam
cat	tan	sad	ham
hat	fan	had	
sat	van	pad	
mat	man		
pat	Dan		

<u>ap</u>	<u>ag</u>	<u>ax</u>
cap	bag	ax
gap	rag	tax
lap	sag	wax
map	wag	Max
nap	tag	
rap		
tap		
zap		

7A. Word Formation

1. Place the short **"a"** vowel card on the table for reference.
2. Download and print our **"ax"** letter cards (or make your own).
3. Teach a says **"a"**, x says **"x"**.
4. Teach **"a"** and **"x"** together say **"ax"**.
5. Teach and show that by moving a letter and placing it in front of **"ax"** that a new word is formed (tax, wax, etc.).
6. Change the beginning letter to form different words.

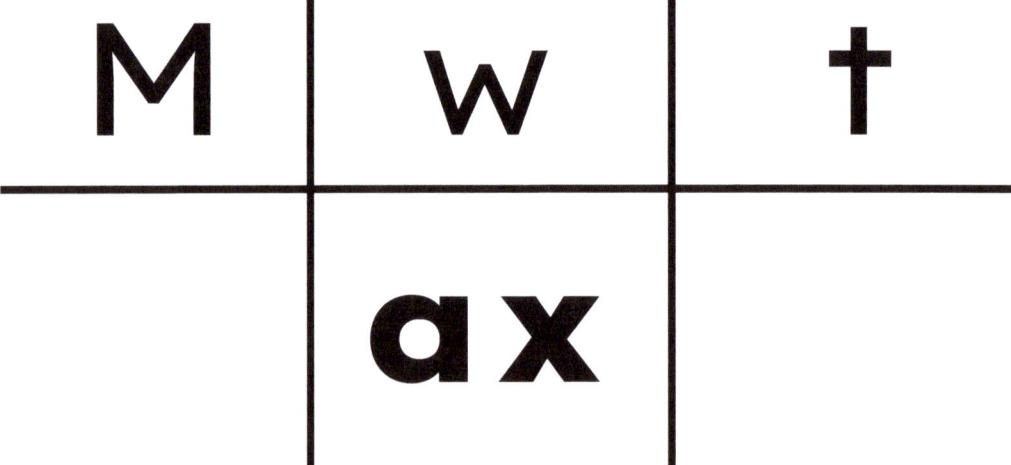

Download and print this activity as a free printable on www.OliKidsCo.com/downloads.

7B. Cup Game

Materials: Plastic cups and permanent markers, or plastic cups, paper, markers, and tape.

1. Using plastic cups, write **"ax"** on one cup (or tape it on). Write or tape each of the following letters on separate cups: **M, w, t**.
2. Instruct the child to find the cup that says **"ax"**.
3. Instruct the child to make the word **"wax"** by finding the correct beginning letter among the remaining cups.
4. If needed, use a different color marker for **"ax"** than for the single letters.
5. Repeat by asking the child to make a new word by changing the first letter of the word to form different words (Max, tax, wax).

7C. Flip Cards Game

Materials: Index cards, markers

1. Write "**ax**" on an index card.
2. Write the letters **M, t, w** on separate index cards.
3. You can use a different color for "**ax**" and a different color for the letters to alleviate any confusion. Example: Write "**ax**" in red and all other letters in black.
4. Place the "**ax**" card on the table.
5. Place all other letter cards in a pile in front of "**ax**".
6. Ask the child to read the first word. Then remove the beginning consonant card, replace it with a new consonant, and have the child read the next word.
7. You may use a timer as a challenge.

7D. Play Match Game

Materials: Index cards, markers

1. Using index cards, write out two cards for each of the words in this lesson (**ax, Max, tax, wax**).
2. You can either play match game with only the words introduced in this lesson or add in words from previous lessons. See the word list to use in games at the beginning of this lesson.
3. Shuffle all of the cards and place them face down on the table so all the words are hidden.
4. Decide which player will go first.
5. Each player will take a turn flipping over two cards and reading the word on each card.
6. When a player gets a match, they keep their cards and have another turn.
7. Cards that don't match get placed back where they were and the second player takes a turn.
8. When no cards remain on the table, the player with the most matches is the winner.

7E. Play Cut Up Words

Materials: Index cards, markers

1. Write a reading word on an index card with space between the letters. Example: w a x
2. Cut the word up so you have 3 pieces.
3. Mix up the letters and ask the child to place the letters in the correct order to spell the word. Example: **"wax"**.
4. Variation: Your child can cut up a word from the **"ax"** word list for you to solve too!
5. You may use any or all of the words you have taught up until this point. Refer to the word list for games included at the beginning of this lesson.

Note Before Moving Ahead

It takes a lot of repetition for new readers to learn to read. Move slightly ahead with the sequential lessons and then back to playing games until all the letter sounds and words are mastered. Repetition is the key. Refer to the short **"a"** vowel card frequently, which should be on the table for all lessons.

Myrtle's Reminder:

New skills take time. Go slow and steady.

Repeat, repeat, repeat!

7F. Mixed Word Practice #1

Directions

1. Point to the words **ax, tax, wax, ax, Max** as you read line #1 on the next page.
2. Ask the child to repeat after you as you read the words again.
3. Ask the child to read each word as you point to each word in a left to right sequence. Assist as needed.
4. As the child makes errors, refer to the short **"a"** vowel card on the table. Remind the child that the letter **"a"** says **"a"** like in apple. Point to the letter **"a"** in each word.
5. The word lists can be cut into strips so that just one line is presented at a time. The word lists can be covered with a blank sheet of paper so that only one line at a time can be seen.
6. Move ahead if these words are mastered, or repeat lessons for repetition.

7F. Mixed Word Practice #1

1. ax tax wax ax Max

2. wag wax tax ham jam

3. Max tax ham tan ran

4. ad bad dad sag tag

5. fan hat sat mad sad

6. tax rag mat pat lap

Checking In

Continue having the child read the word lists and short **"a"** word stories. Continue to play games as needed. Making learning to read into a game format makes learning to read fun. Take the time needed for mastery before moving to the next section.

7G. Mixed Word Practice #2

1. tax wag rag ad had bat

2. tag wax Sam map man ran

3. ham hat Max nap lap mad

4. ax had Sam sag wag bag

5. wax nap dad bad sad had

6. tan jam van pat mat fat

7. ad gap tax ham zap mat

8. lap map sat cat rag tag

7H. Short "a" Sentence Practice

1. Max and Sam had a nap.

2. The cat and Max had a nap.

3. Dad is mad at the fat cat.

4. Sam had a cap and tan bag.

5. Max had a map and a van.

6. Pam and Sam had ham and jam.

7. The tan cat sat on a mat.

8. Dan ran to the van.

Move to the next page to begin the word check.

7I. Word Check

Ask the child to read the listed words on the next page. Use your copy (below) to check off the words read correctly and to take any notes about words that need review.

Use previous word checks again as needed.

	✓	NOTES
1. ax		
2. tax		
3. wax		
4. Max		

7I. Word Check

1. ax
2. tax
3. wax
4. Max

Lesson 8

Learning to Read "ab" Words

> cab   jab   lab   tab

Students learn mastery of the **"ab"** words listed above and reinforce **"at"**, **"an"**, **"ad"**, **"am"**, **"ap"**, **"ag"** and **"ax"** words using the following lessons:

8A. Word Formation
8B. Cup Game*
8C. Flip Cards Game*
8D. Match Game*
8E. Cut Up Words Game*
8F. Mixed Word Practice
8G. Short Sentence Practice
8H. Short Story: Cats Ran
8I. Word Check

*Games 8B, 8C, 8D, and 8E can be played in any order.

Words to Use in Lesson 8 Games

Combine **"at"**, **"an"**, **"ad"**, **"am"**, **"ap"**, **"ag"** and **"ax"** words learned in Lessons 1-7 with **"ab"** words introduced in Lesson 8 to reinforce existing skills and build confidence. As you play Cup Game, Flip Cards Game, Match Game, and Cut Up Words Game, use the following word lists:

<u>at</u>	<u>an</u>	<u>ad</u>	<u>am</u>
at	an	ad	am
bat	can	bad	jam
fat	pan	dad	Pam
rat	ran	mad	Sam
cat	tan	sad	ham
hat	fan	had	
sat	van	pad	
mat	man		
pat	Dan		

<u>ap</u>	<u>ag</u>	<u>ax</u>	<u>ab</u>
cap	bag	ax	cab
gap	rag	tax	jab
lap	sag	wax	lab
map	wag	Max	tab
nap	tag		
rap			
tap			
zap			

8A. Word Formation

1. Place the short **"a"** vowel card on the table for reference.
2. Download and print our **"ab"** letter cards (or make your own).
3. Teach a says **"a"**, b says **"b"**.
4. Teach **"a"** and **"b"** together say **"ab"**.
5. Teach and show that by moving a letter and placing it in front of **"ab"** that a new word is formed (cab, jab, lab, tab).
6. Change the beginning letter to form different words.

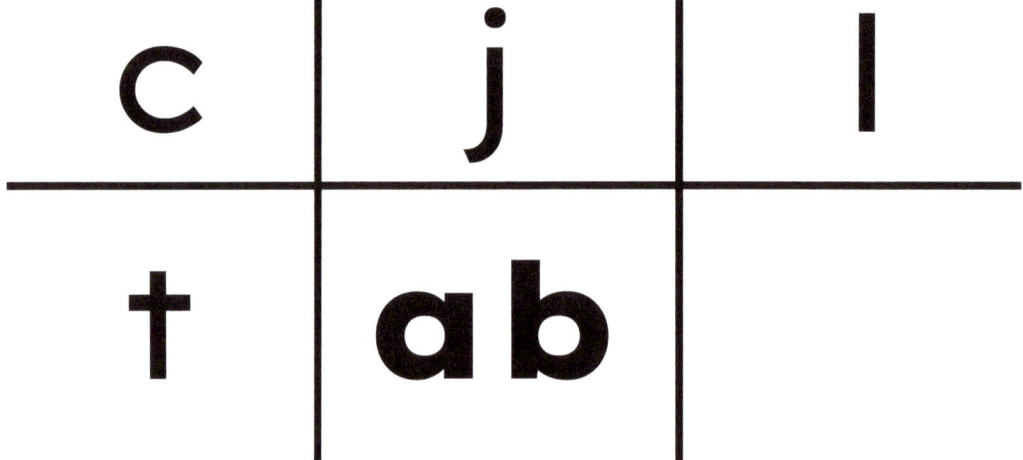

 Download and print this activity as a free printable on www.OliKidsCo.com/downloads.

8B. Cup Game

Materials: Plastic cups and permanent markers, or plastic cups, paper, markers, and tape.

1. Using plastic cups, write **"ab"** on one cup (or tape it on). Write or tape each of the following letters on separate cups: **c, j, l, t**.
2. Instruct the child to find the cup that says **"ab"**.
3. Instruct the child to make the word **"cab"** by finding the correct beginning letter among the remaining cups.
4. If needed, use a different color marker for **"ab"** than for the single letters.
5. Repeat by asking the child to make a new word by changing the first letter of the word to form different words (cab, jab, lab, tab).

8C. Flip Cards Game

Materials: Index cards, markers

1. Write "**ab**" on an index card.
2. Write the letters **c, j, l, t** on separate index cards.
3. You can use a different color for "**ab**" and a different color for the letters to alleviate any confusion. Example: Write "**ab**" in red and all other letters in black.
4. Place the "**ab**" card on the table.
5. Place all other letter cards in a pile in front of "**ab**".
6. Ask the child to read the first word. Then remove the beginning consonant card, replace it with a new consonant, and have the child read the next word.
7. You may use a timer as a challenge.

8D. Play Match Game

Materials: Index cards, markers

1. Using index cards, write out two cards for each of the words in this lesson (**cab, jab, lab, tab**).
2. You can either play match game with only the words introduced in this lesson or add in words from previous lessons. See the word list to use in games at the beginning of this lesson.
3. Shuffle all of the cards and place them face down on the table so all the words are hidden.
4. Decide which player will go first.
5. Each player will take a turn flipping over two cards and reading the word on each card.
6. When a player gets a match, they keep their cards and have another turn.
7. Cards that don't match get placed back where they were and the second player takes a turn.
8. When no cards remain on the table, the player with the most matches is the winner.

8E. Play Cut Up Words

Materials: Index cards, markers

1. Write a reading word on an index card with space between the letters. Example: c a b
2. Cut the word up so you have 3 pieces.
3. Mix up the letters and ask the child to place the letters in the correct order to spell the word. Example: **"cab"**.
4. Variation: Your child can cut up a word from the **"ab"** word list for you to solve too!
5. You may use any or all of the words you have taught up until this point. Refer to the word list for games included at the beginning of this lesson.

Note Before Moving Ahead

It takes a lot of repetition for new readers to learn to read. Move slightly ahead with the sequential lessons and then back to playing games until all the letter sounds and words are mastered. Repetition is the key. Refer to the short **"a"** vowel card frequently, which should be on the table for all lessons.

Myrtle's Reminder:

New skills take time. Go slow and steady.

Repeat, repeat, repeat!

8F. Mixed Word Practice

Directions

1. Point to the words **cab, jab, lab, tab, cab** as you read line #1 on the next page.
2. Ask the child to repeat after you as you read the words again.
3. Ask the child to read each word as you point to each word in a left to right sequence. Assist as needed.
4. As the child makes errors, refer to the short **"a"** vowel card on the table. Remind the child that the letter **"a"** says **"a"** like in apple. Point to the letter **"a"** in each word.
5. The word lists can be cut into strips so that just one line is presented at a time. The word lists can be covered with a blank sheet of paper so that only one line at a time can be seen.
6. Move ahead if these words are mastered, or repeat lessons for repetition.

8F. Mixed Word Practice

1. cab jab lab tab cab

2. jab tab lab cab tab

3. cap cab ham lab map

4. ax tag jab wag man

5. pat sat cab rap tap

6. mad dad sag tab lab

Checking In

Continue having the child read the word lists and short **"a"** word stories. Continue to play games as needed. Making learning to read into a game format makes learning to read fun. Take the time needed for mastery before moving to the next section.

8G. Short "a" Sentence Practice

1. Dad and Sam had a tan van.

2. Dad sat in a cab.

3. Dad is mad at Sam.

4. The cat sat in the hat.

5. Pam had a map.

6. Dan had a nap.

7. Dan and a man had a nap.

8. Max sat in a cab.

8H. Short Story

Cats Ran

Cats ran and ran.
Cats ran to Pam.
Cats ran to Max.
Cats ran to Sam.
Cats sat on the van.

8H. Short Story

Cats sat.

Cats nap, nap, nap.

8I. Word Check

Ask the child to read the listed words on the next page. Use your copy (below) to check off the words read correctly and to take any notes about words that need review.

Use previous word checks again as needed.

	✓	NOTES
1. cab		
2. jab		
3. lab		
4. tab		

8I. Word Check

1. cab
2. jab
3. lab
4. tab

 Download and print this certificate as a free printable on www.OliKidsCo.com/downloads.

Congratulations!

....
Student's Name

Learned to read short "a" words

....
Signed **Date**

See you in Book 2 where we'll learn the following short "e" words:

et

bet
get
jet
let
met
net
pet
set
vet
wet
yet

en

Ben
den
hen
men
pen
ten

ed

bed
fed
led
Ned
red
Ted
wed
Ed

eg/egg

beg
leg
peg
egg

ell

bell
fell
sell
tell
well
yell

es/ess

yes
less
mess
Bess

em

hem